BEAUTIFUL MONSTERS

BOOKS BY STUART HENSON

The Impossible Jigsaw
Ember Music
Clair de Lune (with Mark Bennett)
A Place Apart
The Odin Stone
Feast of Fools (with Bill Sanderson)
The Way You Know It
a Post Card to (with John Greening)
Twelve Days (with Bill Sanderson)

as editor:
John Gohorry: Bold Heart

for children:
Who Can Tell? (Illustrated by Wayne Anderson)

FORTHCOMING

Driving to Bear Lake & Other Stories

BEAUTIFUL MONSTERS

STUART HENSON

Printed by imprintdigital
Upton Pyne, Exeter
www.digital.imprint.co.uk

Typesetting and cover design by The Book Typesetters
hello@thebooktypesetters.com
07422 598 168
www.thebooktypesetters.com

Published by Shoestring Press
19 Devonshire Avenue, Beeston, Nottingham, NG9 1BS
(0115) 925 1827
www.shoestringpress.co.uk

First published 2022
© Copyright: Stuart Henson
© Cover photograph: Kathy Henson

The moral right of the author has been asserted.

ISBN 978-1-915553-16-4

ACKNOWLEDGEMENTS

Acknowledgements are due to the editors of the following publications where some of these poems first appeared: *The Dark Horse*, *The Frogmore Papers*, *The High Window*, *The Hudson Review*, *London Grip*, *The North*, *PN Review*, *Poetry & All That Jazz*, *Raceme*, *The Rialto*, *The Spectator*, *Stand* and *Wild Court*.

'Factory Girls Playing Football' was shortlisted for the Frogmore Prize 2022.

CONTENTS

Wants Out	1
Beautiful Monsters	2
Clouds	3
Tunes for Bears to Dance to	4
Sea Interludes	6
Sea-Holly	7
L'après-midi d'un Phone	8
Aged	10
Hen Harrier	11
The swallows have brought their young…	12
Weeping Widows	13
Marquee	14
Superstore	15
Factory Girls Playing Football	17
The Elephant That Sits on Your Head	18
'Ballbarians'	19
Bookworm	20
The Mad Ambulist of Kentish Town	21
St George & the Princess	22
River Polaroids	23
1 Elvers	23
2 Otters	23
3 Water-Lilies	23
4 Punt	24
5 Canoe	24
6 Lock	24
7 Reed Tugs	25
The Little House on the Fen	26
Dung-Heap	27
Clouds 2	28

At Dawn 29

The book left out 30

Honeysuckle 31

Bees 32

THE ROOFTOPS OF PARIS

Garret 35

Le Buffet 37

Au Cabaret-Vert 38

Ma Bohème 39

Rooks 40

Drinking Alone 41

Encounter 42

Addiction 43

If It Wasn't for Bad Luck, I Wouldn't Have No Luck at All 44

A Pipe 45

DECLINE & FALL

After Tibullus 49

After Suetonius 50

The Villa at Baiae 51

After Martial 52

In the Colosseum 53

WANTS OUT

A honey bee. Butting the double-glass
struck with its baffling transparency.
It holds him back like a force-field,
denial, a mime's plane of impossibility.

I grab a key. An A4 sheet to guide him free
and he skies away gladly above the cotoneaster
into the inexplicable vastness of liberty.

Good use for your poem: saving a bee.
Think of the hives of them—in drawers,
notebooks, anthologies. Tear them all out!
Their noise, their restlessness, humming incessantly...

Think of the planet. Swing clear the casement.
Go with them selflessly into the summer light,
each one a paradigm, freighted with seed.

BEAUTIFUL MONSTERS

Mild as beggars' these hands, these mazed
flailing fronds: Turkish hazels drying along the kerb
like medusas washed up, beached octopi, drowned—
from beyond the undersea bedlam of wind,
eyes popping with pressure of breeding again.

No end to what you might find in this little shop
of wonders. A rock with a world curled inside.
Strewn plane leaves like shavings, or unstuck notes.
Brown medlars maybe, their tawny sphincters
shrinking to mush in the seeds of the rain.

There's cobnuts' fraught brows, and the upturned boats
of sweet chestnuts embroiled in a puzzle of spikes.
Come night there are wings at the street-lights,
your window's alive with a textile of shades—
vexed hour of the moth and its hazardous flight.

Begin, then, with stars and with sand-grains:
to count them all down to the edge of reason.
There's business here for a million lives.
Or better I think to stay still and survive
with this one quince flower in the wrong season.

CLOUDS

But they have no destinations!
How could they—borne on the wind's whist?
Where can they go but chasing the future,
naked, oblivious, skeined out of mist?

Lost on the Second Day, voided of will,
they're vague as mind's foothills, casually
blushed—rushed on at the sun's volition,
restless arrivals, themselves their terminus.

TUNES FOR BEARS TO DANCE TO

'Language is a cracked kettle on which we beat out tunes for bears to dance to, while all the time we long to move the stars to pity.' – Flaubert

$$\left\{ \begin{array}{c} 2 \\ 4 \end{array} \right.$$

Wrong stop. Wrong foot. Wrong turn. Wrong place.
Wrong suit. Wrong time to play the ace.

Wrong man. Wrong church. Wrong vow. Wrong girl.
Wrong speech. Wrong joke. Wrong choice of words.

Wrong house. Wrong street. Wrong door. Wrong day.
Wrong lie. Wrong truth. Wrong every way.

$$\left\{ \begin{array}{c} 3 \\ 4 \end{array} \right.$$

The slap of the stick and the kick of the drum.
The drag of the chain and the strain of the song.
The blood on the sawdust. The weight of the light.
The rime on the straw in the frost-eaten night.

The laughter of children. The pity of whores.
The maggots that creep in the pads of his sores.
The silence of stars as they weep through the black.
The dogs in the box-car. The rats on the track.

The feet without claws and the jaws with no teeth.
The pap in the bucket. The shit-stink of meat.
The pits of his eyes and the depths of his rage.
The rust-roaring stains on the bars of the cage.

$$\left\{ \begin{array}{l} 4 \\ 4 \end{array} \right.$$

Word   weird   wired   welt
Stave   starved   spat   spelt
Tread   tied   toyed   trolled
Step   strap   script   scald

Trip   tap   trope   twist
Jest   just   jerk   gist
Sign   signifier   stress
Paws   parse   pause   press

$$\left\{ \begin{array}{l} 6 \\ 8 \end{array} \right.$$

Under the light of a moon like an old kettle
pitted and potted and made of a soft metal
Bear goes out dancing and beating his tambourine
(mud makes and marks every pace like soft plasticine)

Next day police with their notebooks and spy-glasses
follow his passage through damp woods and salt-marshes—
out to the beach where the trail of his minuet
washes away like a song that the world forgets

SEA INTERLUDES

I

Alone on the seaweed boundary
his thoughts are beginning to run
tide-wise, washed by a light
turned sandy like old Super 8.

Shouts peal; time waits; the wet ball spins
subject to laws no longer governing.
Foam at his heels, the fine grains swim.
He is almost gone, scarcely visible.

Neither out nor in.

II

Mermaids in their mortality
plunged in the swell:
high-riding arms,
a sky of coral.

Wide eyes like seals'
in the sea's bright scales
as the sun sinks
and the light fails.

SEA-HOLLY

for Kevin Crossley-Holland at 80

Forget your laurels take instead this crown:
sea-holly, dry from the dune's head—
spiked, silver, salted, wind-shred.

Sun's aphrodisiac; a beach spread
with its worm-casts, razors,
prints to the waves' edge…

Tread out on tide-glaze; measure
light's flood, and gather in weed-roil,
quartz-glint, prizes like driftwood.

L'APRÈS-MIDI D'UN PHONE
ou si les femmes dont tu gloses…

First thing she did was place it on the glass surface
of the bedside table—maybe just on purpose
to make a point about the other men she'd had.
It did that anyway, vibrating like a mad
hornet at intervals. One time it went off right
at the wrong moment, and it didn't stop all night.
Her inbox seemed to be a veritable nest
of buzzing messages. It was a kind of test
I guess, to see how I'd react. Best to ignore
it I decided and got on with the fore-play.
By turns she was silent and rigid like a sphinx
then liquid, loquacious, slippery as Syrinx.
Sometimes our gasps together, like a melody
breathed on pan-pipes, fell into sync, almost a free
improvisation, loose-structured, ABAB
or frolicked like a *Jeu de Vagues* by Debussy.

Refléchissons…
                    sunlight and secrecy declare
the morning as it creeps toward her underwear
cast in a circlet of dark silks beside the bed,
sloughed like the meshy skin of a snake as it sheds
its outer self and makes a shining artefact
from its bright scales: a rainbow's re-appearing act…

Now in the shower *un flôt antique de lumière*
sets off the thousand limpid droplets on her hair
in *clartés* and *frissons*, and all the while she sings
and soaps, oblivious to the phone that jumps and rings
silently, the urgency of its vibration
disturbing my post-coital doze. Irritation
too insistent to be borne! Who is this lover,
husband, boss? A bore who won't give up. Hand hovers.
It's bad faith to look. I know the screen will bare his
Caller ID… Shall I pick up, spill the affair
while he still gapes aghast—a blow by blow account

of how we'd lick the salt from crevices and mount
each other in unthought-of ways and grip and kiss...?

Instead, I let him grumble inch-wise to his doom
like some poor soul flailing and beating off a swarm
at a cliff's edge—backward above the precipice.

AGED

I'm thinking again of Gallagher's Strat.
You can't get that sweated scrubbed-out look
from a custom shop, and you can't cheat it
home like some shabby-chic with a sanding-block.

Just the road-house hours—in the clubs
with the crowd and the guys with real chops.
And drinking too much. Aye, there's the rub:
once you've slipped down the first the thirst never stops.

Then that night in the ditch looking up
at the stars when he thought it was lost:
tossed out like a fly-tip of building-scrap
and moonlight scaling the frets like frost.

HEN HARRIER

There are forces at work over which he has no control
though he quarters the moor like a satellite scan.
Pick your enemies carefully: it's never a plan
to go head-to-head with your forked *Homo sapiens.*

One for me, one for them—there's an equable deal.
Trouble is, he's not honing his stratagems:
the kill-words like 'vermin' don't seem to occur to him
and he's keeping his distance, aloof from the din.

He drifts like an *éminence grise* in the reservoir's eye,
in the chill wan sun. His lawyers are gathering evidence
but nothing will come out of nothing—an absence.

Will the sky appeal when the judgement's made?
He's no wish to be seen as a ghost-bird—
no care to be numbered among the disappeared.

The swallows have brought their young...

The swallows have brought their young to the brickyard.
The hottest day of the year so far and they sprinkle their chatter,
make graces across the unbroken sky in the shapes of their songs.

On the power-lines, in their cabin-crew uniforms, they're
provisioning for the long haul south through the air-space
of Africa, through the furnace winds and magnetic shifts...

The newest are gobby but grateful. They wait to be fed
or encouraged to try out the wings of the air and its steepness,
the depths and the sweeps of its high slopes and ramps.

They are restless now, on the brink of a passage that proves them
true scions of tribes without teachers or futures or borders or gods.

Our house for a day, and we praise them—their attitude:
their force-field of noise, their delight and their thrust.

WEEPING WIDOWS

Old gold beneath a canopy of gloom.
The month dragging its muddy feet into winter.
Odd hints: the bryony's festivity, twisting
its beady reds up in the twigs—and this

the *lacrymaria* have pitched their tents
among wet grasses where the verges gleam;
a jamboree, a protest camp, networking
messages through loamy screeds.

MARQUEE

A clipper or a galleon
riding the wave of the horizon
leagues out of anywhere

Who beached it there
under the flying clouds
a trim three-master party-craft

decked for the last trimester?
Full stretch of pennants:
England expects no less

God bless this ship of fools
this champagne man-o'-war
blown on a rogue trade

from some distant harbour

SUPERSTORE

In case you're in some doubt they'll make it clear:
what you get here, the signage says, is *CHOICE*
in abundance, the good old *BRITISH*
marketplace where people who care
about these things will know it's *FRESH*
and wholesome fare prepared with *LOVE*.

But yet I worry about 'love'
and how its meaning ceases to be clear
when every Tom, Dick & Saatchi wanting to refresh
a tired brand and influence my choice
uses the word I'd sooner keep for those I care
for deeply. Maybe it's a British

thing: *'No Emotions, Please, We're British!'*
We've always been a little shy about expressing love,
though none the less we ought to care
when someone tarnishes what should shine clear
in a murky world. Yes, if I had the choice
I'd call a moratorium and find fresh

ways of saying it; let's blow a breath of fresh
air in the over-heated space of British
talk and give ourselves the kind of choice
the Inuit are said to have for 'snow'. I'd love
our social speech to be more subtle, clear
and unambiguous, so when the board says *CARE*

I'm puzzled if it's noun or verb: is it the care
they lavish on the cakes—no additives, fresh
eggs and flour? Or is it me, buying with a clear
conscience, showing concern for British
farmers and the welfare of the ones I love?
And then of course that blazoned 'choice'

could be an adjective… It's choice
I'm spoiled for all round. 'Who cares?'
I hear you say. 'It's only words, and love is love
even when language dies. Your simple 'fresh'
has amorous overtones, and as for 'British'
only fools and politicians have that clear.'

British or not, I still set store by words like *love*.
Take care. You have a choice: to keep them fresh
or let them be *REDUCED TO CLEAR.*

FACTORY GIRLS PLAYING FOOTBALL

The lads don't like it but they've commandeered the yard:
wild voices louder than the trucks, pig-killing squeals
and shunting-axle tackles, wind-flung screams.

Ellie keeps goal against the moss-black wall. Janine
rotates her hips, elbows Morela off the ball and sets
Alisha floating down the right toward the bins

where Yasmin's sulking since it's not her turn...
Vicky steps over, lays it off ... and Harsha shoots.
Nobody loses in this game: no-one keeps score.

This is the art of Super League. Three minutes more
before the hooter goes. Soccer's sorority. There are
no substitutes. Hijab's no barrier. Transfers are free.

Only Sunitra, six months scanned, nurses her bump
and watches from behind the canteen's lichened glass
obscured by year on year of tears and soot-fall.

Her daughter—it's a girl—kicks harder now
as if she's keen to get outside and breathe fresh air,
take on the unfair world; start playing football.

THE ELEPHANT THAT SITS ON YOUR HEAD

'Class is so often the atmosphere in the room. It's there in a nonchalant comment,
in a sequence of cues and signals that can only be parsed by those in the know...'

No, ignorance is never bliss.
It burns when someone takes the piss
out of your Burton tie: *That piece of sack!*
or pats you on the back for your mistake
of giving Shakespeare's Antony an H.
Or loaning you a book she smiles
Take care of it. Don't scuff the jacket!
All you can do is nod and hack it
while you suffocate. Too late:
the elephant squats on your life.
You gag on shibboleths.
You check which knife...

'BALLBARIANS'

Gladiators of taws and alleys!
Who wouldn't swap pockets of gems
for steel—temper of rolled-down borders
detonator of craters-full of winking glass?
Worth ten good wins in any scrap.
Only the hard men had them, clunking
and irreducible: score-settlers, Parliamentarians
lords of the battle-grounds.
They knew the price of victories.
What makes the world go round.

BOOKWORM

is inside the text
and I mean that literally
though white space
seems as tasty and he
appears to read backward
or AC/DC

takes time
and goes randomly
between lines or he mines
the periphery—a maggot
a minuscule penis a dreamer
who may never be

a wise fly or a moth
and what he digests might
be dust at its best or just
jottings of madness
or nothing
but poetry

THE MAD AMBULIST OF KENTISH TOWN

Flat-cap, a paper bag, a covid mask:
that sudden unsettling sense of déjà-vu.
You've seen this man before who's striding past,
power-walking, pacing with intent,
almost escaping down the station's length.

He's counting steps and measuring the length
of platforms 2 and 3, head up, intent
on leaving what's behind him in the past,
oblivious to our time-slipped point-of-view,
in his cap, with his bag and his outlaw's mask.

ST GEORGE & THE PRINCESS

Worldly and otherworldly: the Principessa and St George,
the horse's rump stone-white and sweaty, stuck between.
Stage left, his page, a ghosted lance, and one doomed sheep.
Beyond is Trebizond, Moorish and intricate as scrimshaw.
And right, the dragon feeling moreish too and breathing out
miasma of decay that rots gold leaf to lichen green and sepia.
George mounting, while his patient dog watches the dragon
thrashing like some angry croc on the farther shore.
George knows the creature's nothing but a metaphor.
But why the gallows, up, behind him, square, no Calvary,
the victims debagged mockingly for the town to cheer?
Tomorrow and the next day's sacrifice? Or runaways?
Hard times need iron discipline, from the top down—
no-one exempt, Princess nor King nor minister.
No thieves in Jacobus. It could be petty larceny, dissent,
or something altogether crueller and more sinister.

RIVER POLAROIDS

1 Elvers

The weirs are a constant threshing, restless
like white noise magnified, a factory
of foam and ozone with a long dark boom
nudging the current where it forces by.

And three-inch elvers made of rusty slime
meshed through the tumble and the weed-clung brick.
Jars of the river's protozoic murk: life
on the margin, marginal, scaling it inch by inch.

2 Otters

Now otters are back on the Great Ouse.
When I was small they'd gone; only
my Grandad told the story of the shape
that nosed into his fishing tent one night

while he was far away and half awake
and puzzled what it was that broke his dream.
It slipped back quickly then, a summer's ghost,
setting a shimmer down the river's gleam.

3 Water-Lilies

Lilies go deep, the weed deeper.
The current trawls beneath them both
as a dream will, to drown the sleeper.

4 Punt

The big square cushions flump down on the boards
and Skipper Hall steps back, hands you the rope.
The boatyard rocks a little; you push out.
Your paddles dip, stirring the river's soup.

Below the bridge the surface cuts up lightly
like a file. And through its gape, parting a wave
a cabin-cruiser thrusts on to the lock.
Arched shadows broaden like inverted smiles.

5 Canoe

Canvas and lath, a Sopwith of the stream.
Life-jacket like a pilot's bright Mae-West.
Twin paddles dripping right and left.
Gliding a prayer. Bound to go down.

The creeping cold of water in your seat
says time to ditch. Pram-wheels drag home.
Now it's *For Sale* in the local rag.
Bought for a tenner. Sold for twelve pounds.

6 Lock

Two wooden gates that leaked persistently
and the sluice, a huge slow-motion guillotine.
A hydrostatic miracle that raised a boat
twelve feet from shadow into clarity.

Crank-handle's yelp, the steady heave,
then chugged exhaust, gates' bump, weed-churn…
before the hulls slip out, away from us.
Behind, the lock's dark flood, its oily sheen.

7 Reed Tugs

My father made them from a twist of reed
spiralled around itself, the thin end tucked
and tied-in like a rope, the fat part kinked
up for a smokestack, glossy, racing-green.

We set them off and watched them circle
wallow, catch in foam, upturn and travel
onward keeled by their plunging periscopes.
Half raft then, funnel-less. Half submarines.

*

THE LITTLE HOUSE ON THE FEN

Like linnets. A cage too small.
We live below huge skies—
under their storm weight,
among feet in the scrabbling thatch
in the spiders' gaze
with a pump and a tap.
Our days are whipped up
and they rattle away
like the grains of the land.
By night when the temperatures drop
all that's black seeps in.
Our dawns are opaque and shapeless
and flooded with sun.
I gave this woman my troth
and twelve shillings a week.
She cooks. The range sputters
with carrots and carcasses.
One flesh on the slender laths
of our bones. Two souls
in the cabbage scents of our skins.

DUNG-HEAP

A gift, from the yard to the field,
still steamy with byre nights and the reek
of cow-piss and trodden splat—
payback for a soil they've knackered
with spray-lines, pumped fatter on nitrogen.

Let it rest, then, and dream of grass
breathing and thick tongues rasping
and bees deep among thistle-knots.
Let it settle and dry, a mound for the crows
to crow on, for worms to go mining in.

This way fertility: your circle of sunshine
and slather and green rain in prints.
Shade-lapped by the last low rays it's
a cordillera, a reef, teeming a million
small brown flies and misted with heat.

CLOUDS 2

Migration of clouds, grazing the blue like buffalo.
Their backs absorb the morning sun as they gaze
westward along their endless skies.
Herd-breath. Heat haze in thin disguise.
Bright mirage-mesas where slow mountains rise.

AT DAWN

Ah! Two cock blackbirds
facing it out on the lawn
like nineteenth-century duellists
in their frock coats,
their beaks a pair of pistols;
Onegin and Lensky, masculine, irresistible,
determined on dignity.
Now *cherchez la femme*.
She watches, lofty in the cherry tree,
quite suitably Victorian and plain,
and plump with lust and sobriety.

A world so darkly civilised
it's almost ours.
Reflect: tomorrow neither will have died;
the loser will forget his pride
and both will beat their pistols into flutes
to greet the sunrise.

THE BOOK LEFT OUT

absorbs
its first September mist

the print lifts imperceptibly
toward
a tall and passive sky.

Each morning words
breathe in
the falling temperatures

leaves pale and curl
as the pages dry...

HONEYSUCKLE

wears her perfume like a country girl—
so blameless and so thick it sweeps
you down the lane of night
into her unconstrained embrace.

Her kiss is deep and chastely amorous;
she winds your senses, weeds your strength.
Who might resist? A priest, a celibate?
She'd give you everything for love's sweet sake.

BEES

Among the long yellow racemes of laburnum
you may discern them mumbling in numbers
on subjects and burdens that seem to perturb them:
of summer and seasons—time's reasons—*ad infinitum*

The Rooftops of Paris

GARRET
(Théophile Gautier)

Low on the tiles a tomcat,
stalking the birds at the bath
on my balcony. Beyond, a garret
that for the sake of art

is framed exactly by two soil-pipes.
If I wanted to please I suppose
I'd place a vase right there
in the window, full of sweet-peas.

And picture for you Roxette
striking a pose with a brush
in her speckled mirror that reflects
an image of not-quite-enough.

Or Margy in just bra and pants
leaning out into the sun
with a bottle she decants
in slow dribbles on her pot-geranium.

Or the young poet maybe
who numbers anxiously his dry syllabics
to please his prof, earn his degree,
and scans for a theme the rooftops of Paris.

Sadly, the true view's more prosaic:
no vines on the window-frame
but rot, flaked paint and a mosaic
of soot that deckles the panes.

For your tart, your artist,
waitress, waiter, widower
there's no charm in being piss-
poor, the opera's tragic character.

One time there might have been
room here for love on a horse-hair
bed below the tiles—a dream
quick-breathing up the narrow stair.

But romance needs its *mise-en-scène:*
some central-heating and silk sheets,
four-poster luxury, thick carpet when
you step out to the tiled *en-suite*.

And now at night the prospect's black.
Roxette's out late, gone dirty-dancing;
and Margy won't be stumbling back
before the sun comes glancing in.

A while since, the poet gave up on
his soaring for the perfect line,
became a hack. Bored then, he traded-in
Parnassus for an office and a mezzanine.

But still this view is all I've got:
my window-on-the-world, something
to watch: one lean old woman and the cat
she teases idly with a ball of string.

LE BUFFET
(Rimbaud)

A broad oak cupboard, ancient and mellowed,
aged dark like some nonagenarian.
Say *Open Sesame!* its odours flow
from its shades, uncorked like a long-stored wine.

Stuffed full. A grave of memories and griefs:
a Christening robe, a scarf, the crumbling lace
on a collar, and grandma's handkerchiefs,
embroidered birds, ribbons and heading-tape.

Reach in and take a medal or a lock
of fine blonde hair, an edelweiss in Baltic
amber, scented like fruit or wedding-cake…

Door to the past, its hinges groan and ache
to tell the stories that it may not speak,
neither for you, nor them, nor old times' sake.

AU CABARET-VERT

(Rimbaud)

Five in the evening

For a week I'd scuffed my shoes in the rough
dust of the highways, walking to Charleroi.
At the Green Man I stopped, asked for a crust—
a ham sandwich—and a mug of Stella.

Stretched out my feet under a green table
and studied the quirks of the pub décor.
And then—almost more than I was able
to bear—the barmaid: huge tits and eyes like stars.

Well, she'd be up for it, no doubt of that!
Look when she brings my sandwich how she pouts,
as if to say I'm yours—and on a plate.

Pink ham and mustard, scented with a clove
of garlic. A frothing pint. It must be love!
Gold sun-rays glinting like the night to come.

MA BOHÈME
(Rimbaud)

I'm stepping out, hands in my torn pockets,
(Still working the coat for that lived-in look)
Me and Calliope, riding the rocket
of imagined love, the road an open book.

Holes in my only jeans, hooking my thumbs
into my belt and steering by the stars;
singing the sky my songs, pulling out plums
of rhyme for the Pleiades, the Great Bear...

The constellations rustle when you sit alone
crouched in the verge some slow September night
and let the dew soak up and through your bones.

I'll make my poems from the beat of headlights,
lulled like some Orpheus by thrumming tyres,
boot-laces plucked against my heart—my lyre.

ROOKS
(Rimbaud)

When winter chokes the meadows
watch them wait,
neutral as undertakers,
angels of shadow,
set to sweep in
from the skies on crepe wings.

Ice in their nests,
mud-laden brooks...
Only their dry caarks
creak round the frost's
ramparts, sifted snow,
dull acres where they come and go.

Flocks wheel the fields of France
perch on each cross—
last season's dead lost
in their cemeteries. Answer
the traveller then, his memory,
black acolytes of death and duty!

Or spare at least, dark saints
churched in the oaks,
songbirds and larks, shouters of hope—
for those who brace against
wood's vacancy, horizon's blast:
men with no future and no past.

DRINKING ALONE

(Baudelaire – Le Vin du solitaire)

That look of singular desire, that rare
unfiltered signalling of sex in the eyes
of the girl who glides past, shoulders bare
as the moon in a lake—cool, undisguised…

The last stack of chips in the gambler's hand;
lewd kisses from my skinny mistress Adeline
or half-heard music from a distant bandstand
wheedling, insistent like some cry of pain…

Nothing to you, my bottle of delights
pregnant with inspiration, joys that might
uplift a poet's heart against all odds.

You pour out hope, pride, youthfulness and life:
a beggar's treasure and the one device
to recreate us, fearless as the gods!

ENCOUNTER
(Baudelaire – À une passante)

Traffic was howling in my ears and eyes
that moment when we passed—she in her slim
black dress, a gloved hand tugging up the hem—
and for one instant all things clarified.

Those slo-mo seconds in a film when fate
throws two together and the soundtrack dims
and he looks back, feeling the weight of time
as it stands still and she moves on. Too late!

Lightning, then night. Lost beauty. Happiness
glimpsed and snatched back—as if a wave had crashed
and took our footprints from us as its wash withdrew.

Where can we meet now but eternity?
Ghost-voice I call out to her silently:
Woman I could have loved you—and you knew!

ADDICTION
(Baudelaire – Le Jeu)

Stretched on their tired chaises-longues, the ancient whores:
too much foundation, too much rouge, they ooze
a feral scent of sweat and musk; their eyes
hollow, compelling; rattling cheap rhinestones in thin ears.

Around the baize their lipless faces glimmer,
cratered like moons, and their arthritic claws
stretch eagerly to grasp the dice, the wheel's shimmer,
and stuff slim pickings down torn bustiers.

Lamps swing pale saucers from the sooted beams,
too weak to cast more than a yellow stain
across the brows of geniuses who prostitute their poems
of love and truth for something more mundane.

It's here like Dante in his reverie
you'll find me, guideless and silent, seated alone
in a corner, leaning and shivering
on my elbows, needing to be at one

with all this demi-monde that passion grips;
envious, yes envious, of the old tarts
and their beaux who long ago gave up
their self-respect and sold the secrets of their hearts.

I choke and drown here in the lives of men
who stumble on toward a precipice.
The fever in their blood's their only sin,
who'll take this fleshly hell before the black abyss.

IF IT WASN'T FOR BAD LUCK, I WOULDN'T HAVE NO LUCK AT ALL

(Baudelaire – Le Guignon)

Who says you make your own luck?
You need the strength of Sisyphus
to keep on rolling that old rock uphill.
Ars longa, vita brevis. True enough!

A crib in Poet's Corner's what you get
for being famous, looming large.
Well, that or nothing for your hours of sweat,
your heart-blood pounding like a funeral march.

Console yourself: your verses shine
like diamonds in abandoned mines,
gold nuggets in a hidden seam.

Meadows blow soft, unheeded
on the cheek of night. Sweet weeds!
The woods write sonnets. Deserts dream.

A PIPE

(Baudelaire)

Dark-grained as a statue from Africa,
I am the author's best pipe.
Look and it's obvious: my life's
shared with a professional smoker.

I am his chimney and his hearth,
his one-man domesticity.
When he's downcast by the vicissitudes
of living, I'm blessedness at last.

His daydreams rise in skeins of blue:
the floating islands of his soul.
Banked in the embers of my bowl

they glow, the bright hopes of his youth.
I am his solace, his relief from pain.
I set his heart on fire again.

Decline & Fall

AFTER TIBULLUS

And this is Livia's bench, this warm stone
altar where she sat and watched Tiberius' return
along the straight Flaminia.

This is a place that you might dedicate
to love-not-strong-enough, that gave her up
to *force majeure*.

She who became most pure of Roman matriarchs
learned patience here, wived to survival and necessity,
and let her gaze stretch out

across the Tiber where bleached bodies bloat—
its long green valley and beyond the aqueduct the heat haze
and the road's red dust...

Yes, this is Livia's bench, warm in the sun, though shadows
darken like spilt wine—and cherry blossom
shreds down heedlessly

spun loose through time.

AFTER SUETONIUS
(The Death of Thrasyllus)

The death of Thrasyllus occurred in this wise.
The sun rising on the Bay of Naples,
he breakfasted among the vines and figs.
Those days, his last, Tiberius would seldom
let his counsellor stray from his company,
and plied him often with demands to say
what things might come to pass when he was gone.
'In ten years' time,' the sage would smile, 'nothing
will change—and everything. Tiberius
will rule and Rome will bow to his bidding.'
This seemed to satisfy the gouty prince
whose breath wheezed from his fat lips and whose fat
fingers shredded a woodlark from its bones.
'No man can tell the hour of his death
but each will recognise the messenger
that brings the news.' And this made Caesar laugh:
'I shall outlive you all—become a god.'
Thrasyllus smiled again. 'Death is a tax
all emperors must pay back to the ruled.
True sons receive their bounty from his will.'
A cloud passed on the terrace and a chill
blew momentarily across the sea.

And then the sun returned. The breeze eased down.
A lizard poked its head between two stones.
Tiberius was sick into a bowl.
A slave boy took it and he wiped his chin.

Then like a twitch the lizard ran across
the table where the old men sat and stopped
there motionless again, its whiplash tail
wrapped round Thrasyllus' finger like a ring.
The sage breathed deeply and he dropped his head.
He closed his eyes. The lizard darted on.

THE VILLA AT BAIAE

Why would you bring water, Bassus, to irrigate
a camomile lawn, your margins of box and myrtle?
Wouldn't give a fig for long avenues of planes
if I could have this, a farm that's over-run
with pigs, its corners chocked with amphorae
that glow with their years of hay-sweet harvest.

November drifts away here. Faustinus' old
retainer and his wife potter among late grapes
Out on the hillside the ageing bull bellows
and locks horns with his usurper. The cocks strut
in the walled garden—nothing to do but copulate!
The dovecote's soothing as snowfall. The light's
grainy like spilt corn. More than enough
for the clattering pigeons, partridges, peahens…

Lares and penates: the gods in the logs
that blaze all night, gilding the gipsy faces
of the children ripe with their giggling mischief.
Even the guests muck-in. The shooting-party
mends the nets; girls from the city take
their turns in bottling fruit; eunuchs steep plums.

When it's all done, the neighbours come
with honeycombs, Sassinian cheese, presents
of dormice, capons, bleating kids: feasting enough
for Senator and bondman, tenant and fattore.
Poor Bassus! Your towers aren't ivory
but they might as well be. Call your sommelier
demand the vintage, quails' eggs, caviar…
You can't order a sunset from Fortnum & Mason.

AFTER MARTIAL
(Epigrams 9:32)

I want a slut: fur coat and no knickers
who fucks my chauffeur first downstairs,
whose ice-cream tongue likes what it licks,
turns tricks for fun, who couldn't care...
I want a girl who'll share the fourth couch in a threesome
not some indecent bit that harps on cash,
makes out she's posh. Leave her
to politicians, toffs—so please 'em.

IN THE COLOSSEUM

Daedalus

Poor criminal Daedalus, rudderless, beating the air.
Now made a treat for us—and six hungry bears!

Two Gladiators

Half shout for Myrinus, half for his foe.
It's fifty-fifty! How will it go?
Please one? Please all? Without hesitation
Caesar condemns them both. Such witty equivocation!

The Spectacle of Pasiphaë

Is it true Pasiphaë fancied a bull?
I think it must be. At Caesar's will
we see it enacted. Bestial. Painful.

The Bubalus

Seems that not one of us
knows what a bubalus
looked like or what it said.
Once it was ponderous. Now it's dead.

Diana as Midwife

The she-boar whelps, torn in her death throes
by a spear's caesarean. Out of the lost, life!
What more will cruel chance disclose?

Synchronised Swimming

Nereids more disciplined than centuries
sport in the waves. You could believe
in mermaids, Triton, all the impossibilities
taught them by Thetis—or Caesar's functionaries.

Rhinoceros

Your creature, Caesar, bursts like a dust-storm
into the arena. Armoured in anger, crazed
with the crowd's rapture, it tosses bulls
like so many balls. Its keepers have taunted
it raw and it's goaded by hatred.
One-horned. Explosive. Impossible. Fated.

NOTES

L'Après-midi d'un Phone: All the quotations are from Mallarmé's poem.

The Elephant that Sits on Your Head: The epigraph is from an essay 'The Atmosphere in the Room' by Ralph Webb that appeared in *The Poetry Review* 110:1 (Spring 2020).

St George & the Princess and the other creatures can be found above an arch in the church of Santa Anastasia, Verona—in a fresco by Pisanello.

The book left out was David Morley's excellent *The Gypsy & the Poet* which the author placed on the grave of John Clare after a reading in Helpstone.

The Rooftops of Paris: My versions of Gautier, Baudelaire and Rimbaud. They try to retain the forms of the originals—and their spirit—but they take more liberties than the word 'translations' would strictly allow. Some of them were included in the French special issue of *The High Window*, December 2020, edited by Timothy Adès.

After Tibullus: Albius Tibullus 'seems to have lived quietly on his estate near Rome, writing pastoral poetry' at the time of Augustus. A friend of Horace and Ovid, he left two books of poems and contributed to one which includes *Sulpicia's Garland*. 'Whether these are by a genuine Roman poetess is impossible to say.' This poem first appeared under the title 'After Tacitus' in *The Hudson Review* Vol LXXIV No 4 (Winter 2022). Whether it's a genuine reproduction of Tibullus is impossible to say.

The Villa at Baiae: A very rough copy of Martial's epigram III lviii

In the Colosseum: Loosely from Martial's *Liber Spectaculorum*.